Sailing

FOR KIDS

Sailing
FOR KIDS

Gary & Steve Kibble

**Photographs by
Tim Hore & Dave Holland**

WILEY NAUTICAL

www.wileynautical.com

First published 1987 as *The Prudential Book of Sailing* by
Reprinted January 2008 by John Wiley & Sons Ltd
The Atrium, Southern Gate, Chichester,
West Sussex, PO19 8SQ, England.
Tel 01243 779777
Email (For orders and customer service enquires): cs-books@wiley.co.uk
Website: www.wileynautical.com

ISBN 978-0906-75477-1

3 9547 00351 2303

Acknowledgements

The publishers would like to thank Neil Bradshaw of the Prudential
Assurance Co. for his support and assistance; Weir Wood Sailing Club
for providing facilities for photography, and Victoria Hounsfield and
Gary Kibble for sailing the boats; John Driscoll of the RYA for his
valuable advice on the manuscript.

The cover photograph is by Champion Photography and the cover design
is by Simon Balley.

Design by PanTek, Maidstone
Composition by A & G Phototypesetters, Knaphill

Contents

1 A first sail   6
2 What is it called?   10
3 Rigging   12
4 Faster gear   15
5 Launching   16
6 Reaching   19
7 Beating   22
8 Tacking   26
9 Running   28
10 Gybing   30
11 Sailing a circular
   course   32
12 Safety   33
13 Capsizing   34
14 Landing   36
15 What makes your
   boat sail?   38
16 Knots   40
17 The rules   41
18 Going faster   42
19 What's next?   47

1   A first sail

For your first sail, choose a warm day with a light wind. Wear warm clothes with an anorak. Put old plimsolls on your feet. Do *not* wear wellington boots because they may fill with water. And remember: ALWAYS WEAR A WELL-FITTING BUOYANCY AID OR LIFEJACKET.

If it is cold, or you are sailing on the sea, wear a wet suit.

On top, wear an overall to keep the wind out. Socks and sailing shoes will keep your feet warm.

Always wear a buoyancy aid or lifejacket.

When you are sailing, you sit facing the sail. Hold the piece of wood (**tiller**) in your back hand. Hold the rope (**mainsheet**) in your front hand. Sit far enough forward to keep your body out of the way of the tiller.

You use the tiller to steer.

1 Push the tiller to turn one way.

2 Pull it to turn the other way.

3 Put the tiller in the middle to go straight ahead.

Pull in the mainsheet to pull in the sail. This makes the boat go faster.

Let out the mainsheet to let out the sail. This makes the boat go slower.

Apart from the mainsheet and tiller, there is one more control. The piece of board that stops the boat slipping sideways is the **daggerboard**. For the time being, sail with it right down.

Now you are ready for your first sail. Set off with the wind coming across the side of the boat. Sail along until you want to turn round. Then push the tiller *away* from you. The boat will turn and the sail will swing over. (Mind your head!) Sit on the other side of the boat. Change hands on the mainsheet and tiller. Put the tiller in the middle of the boat and sail back.

1   Sail with the wind coming across the side of the boat.

2   Turn by pushing the tiller away. Change sides and change hands.

3   Now centre the tiller and sail back.

Stopping

To stop, let go of the mainsheet. If you are in trouble, let go of everything.

Pull in the mainsheet to get going again.

1   This boat has stopped because it is pointing into the wind. It is *in irons*.

2   Push the sail out and push the tiller the other way.

3   The boat will go backwards.

4   Then she will turn.

5   Let go of the sail.

6   Sail off.

2   What is it called?

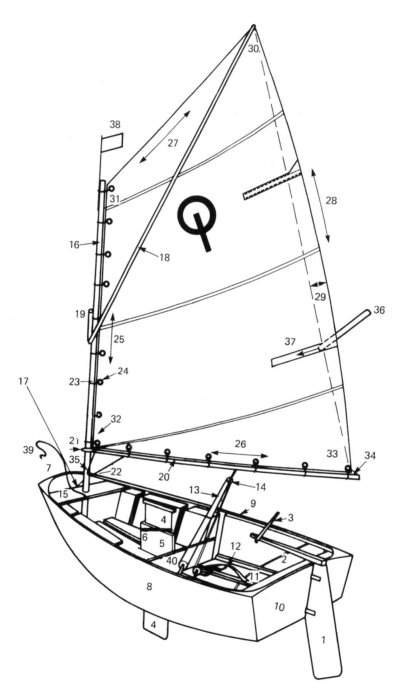

On the opposite page is an Optimist dinghy. The main parts of the boat are labelled. How many do you know? Start by trying to remember the ones in **bold type**. You will soon learn them all.

1	**Rudder**	23	**Sail tie**
2	**Tiller**	24	Cringle (hole)
3	Tiller extension	25	Luff
4	**Daggerboard**	26	Foot
5	Daggerboard case	27	Head
6	Daggerboard elastic	28	Leech
7	**Bow**	29	Roach
8	Side	30	Peak
9	Gunwale	31	Throat
10	**Transom**	32	Tack
11	Buoyancy	33	Clew
12	Toe strap	34	**Outhaul**
13	**Mainsheet**	35	Cleat for kicking strap (vang)
14	Block	36	**Batten**
15	Mast thwart	37	Batten pocket
16	**Mast**	38	**Burgee**
17	Mast securing line	39	**Painter** (should be 4 metres long)
18	**Sprit**	40	Midship beam
19	Sprit adjuster		
20	**Boom**		
21	**Boom jaw**		
22	**Kicking strap (vang)**		

If you have a racing boat, your gear may be a bit different.

3 Rigging

1 Lay out your gear.

2 Now you are ready to rig the boat.

3 Clip the boom jaw on to the mast. Position it so the sail is above the band.

4 Fasten the first sail tie around the boom, using a reef-knot.

5 Do the same with the other sail ties. Don't make them too tight.

6 Tie the sail to the end of the boom with the outhaul rope.

7   Now tie the sail tightly to the mast, using the longer sail ties.

8   Tie the sail to both eyes near the top of the mast. (One tie holds the sail to the mast. The other stops the sprit pulling the sail up.)

9   Fix the burgee to the top of the mast.

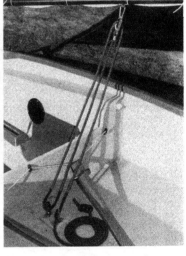

10   Push the battens into their special pockets in the sail. Point the boat into the wind.

11   Fold up the boom and put the mast into the hole in the mast thwart.

12   Attach the mainsheet to the boom.

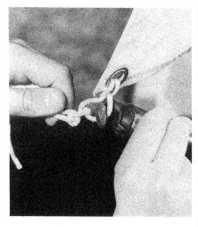

13   Tie the sail to the top of the sprit.

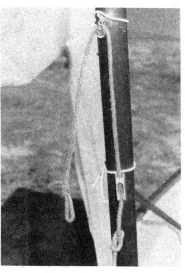

14   Put the bottom of the sprit into the loop of the sprit adjuster.

15   Tighten the rope until creases run from the top of the sprit to the boom jaw.

16   Ask a friend to help you tighten the kicking strap (vang).

17   Here the kicking strap (vang) is tight and has been cleated.

18   Tie the mast into the boat, otherwise it may fall out if you capsize. Finally, put the rudder and daggerboard into the boat. Now you are ready to go sailing!

4 Faster gear

This burgee is held in place by strips of bike inner tube.

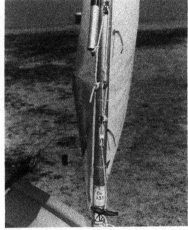

This sprit has an arrangement so it can be adjusted easily while sailing.

This rope (arrowed) stops the boom being pulled down by the kicking strap (vang).

This mainsheet is fixed to a strop (arrowed) which stops the boom bending too much.

This outhaul is adjustable so the curve in the foot of the sail can be altered.

This loop of elastic (arrowed) keeps the daggerboard in position. It also angles the daggerboard towards the rear (aft).

5 Launching

Launching from a windward shore

If the wind is blowing from the shore to the water, you will be launching from a **windward shore**. Take care, the wind will be stronger when you get away from the land. And if you get into trouble, the wind will blow you away from the shore.

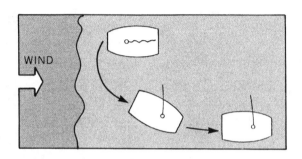

If it is safe to go sailing, launch like this:

1   Lay the daggerboard and rudder in the bottom of the boat.

2   Tie the boat to the trolley and wheel them into the water.

3   Hold the painter (rope) and push the boat off the trolley. Ask a friend to take the trolley.

4   Swing the boat round and get in.

5   Clip on the rudder.

6   Push the daggerboard halfway into its case.

Launching from a leeward shore

This time the wind is blowing from the water on to the shore. It may be difficult to launch into the wind and waves. But if you are in trouble, you will always be blown back to the land.

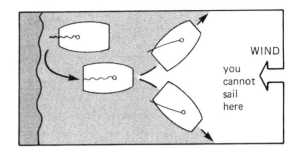

WIND

you cannot sail here

1 Rig the boat, but unclip the mainsheet. Lay the rudder and daggerboard in the bottom of the boat. Wheel the boat into the water.

2 Push the boat off the trolley.

3 Ask a friend to take the trolley.

4 Turn the boat until it points into the wind. Clip on the mainsheet.

5   Push the boat into deeper water. Clip on the rudder.

6   Choose the direction in which you will sail. Push off and get in.

7   Quickly push the daggerboard into its case (but not so far that it hits the bottom).

8   Pull in the mainsheet. Sail off, as close to the wind as you can.

6 Reaching

Reaching is fun! It's fast and easy to control.

What is reaching?

These boats (right) are reaching. They are sailing so the wind comes across the side of the boat. In other words, they are sailing across the wind.

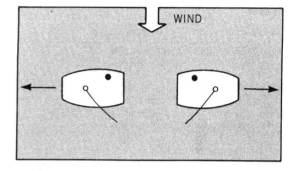

Where is the wind?

You can tell the direction of the wind by looking at your burgee, flags, smoke or ripples on the water. Also if you unclip your mainsheet, the sail will blow away from the wind.

Adjusting the sail

Don't forget that you can control your speed with mainsheet. Pull it in to go faster. Let it out to go slower. Let it go completely to stop (you are then **hove to**).

To adjust the mainsheet for maximum speed keep a straight course.

Let out the mainsheet until the front edge of the sail begins to flap.

Then pull in the sail until it just stops flapping. As you sail along, do this so the sail is always properly adjusted.

Where to sit when reaching

Sit in the boat just behind the midship beam.

If the wind is strong, sit on the side (*gunwale*) to balance the boat.

Steering

Hold the tiller gently, and make only small movements. Otherwise the boat will turn too quickly.

Daggerboard

If you are a beginner, push the daggerboard right down and leave it there. As you get better you can pull the daggerboard halfway up when you are reaching.

Gusts

The water looks dark as a gust travels over it.

When a gust hits the boat, lean back (**hike out**). If the boat still tips over (**heels**), let the mainsheet out a bit.

Don't let a gust turn the boat. Be firm with the tiller and sail in the direction *you* want.

Changing course

Practise sailing across the wind. This is a **beam reach**.

Push the tiller away from you, then straighten up. You are now sailing closer to the wind. You are on a **close reach**. You will have to pull in the sail a bit to stop it flapping.

Now pull the tiller towards you. Straighten up and sail on a **broad reach**. The wind is coming over the corner of the transom. You can let out the sail quite a lot before the front edge flaps.

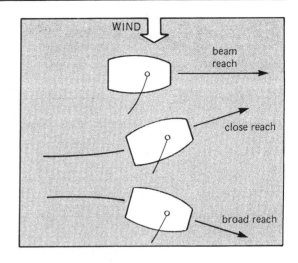

You can sail fast on a reach!

7 Beating

You can't sail straight into the wind. If you try the boat just stops. The only way to sail against the wind from A to B is to **beat**. This means sailing a zig-zag course towards the wind.

This boat is beating

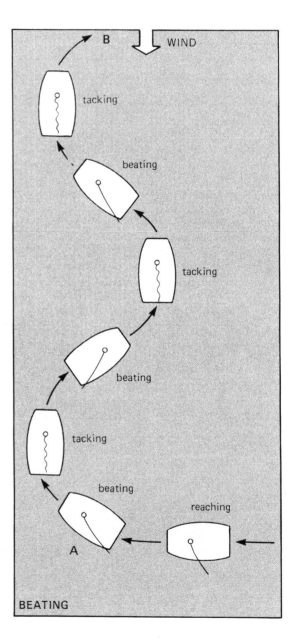

1 To beat, begin on a reach.

2 Pull in the mainsheet until the boom is over the aft corner of the boat (the *quarter*).

3 Now push the tiller away so you turn slowly towards the wind. Watch the front (*luff*) of the sail.

4 When it begins to flap, turn back a little.

5 Straighten up. You are now sailing as close to the wind as you can.

6 Sail on for a little.

7   Then turn towards the wind again. Try to use the tiller so the sail is nearly flapping.

8   Keep the mainsheet pulled in all the time.

9   Push the tiller away. The boat will turn and the sail will swing across. Now beat the other way.

Where to sit when beating

1   Sit so your front leg touches the midship beam.

2   If you are too far back the stern will drag through the water.

3   If you are too far forward, the bow will dig in.

Daggerboard

You must push the daggerboard right
down for beating. Otherwise the boat
will drift sideways.

**1 Use your weight to
balance the boat.**

**2 As the wind gets
stronger sit on the side.**

**3 Any more wind and
you should think about
leaning out (*hiking*).**

8 Tacking

If you turn into the wind and go on turning until the boom crosses the boat, you have tacked (turned round).

Tacking is safe and quite slow. So it is the easiest way to turn round. The pictures show how it's done.

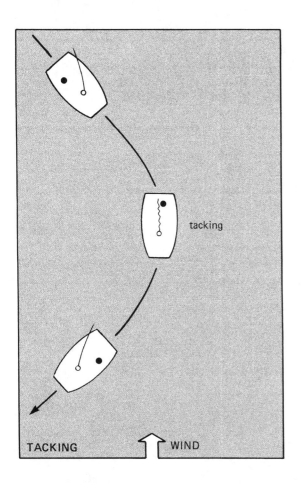

tacking

TACKING   WIND

1 Pick up some speed. Push the tiller away from you and keep it there throughout the turn.

4 You should still have the mainsheet and tiller in your 'old' hands, with the tiller behind your back.

2   As the sail flaps, duck under the boom, facing forwards.

3   The boom and sail will swing across to the other side of the boat.

5   Bring your mainsheet hand to the tiller and use it to hold the tiller as well. Then grab the mainsheet with your 'old' tiller hand.

6   Pull in the mainsheet. Well done, you have tacked!

9 Running

A boat sailing away from the wind is **running**. It is blown along like a feather on a pond.

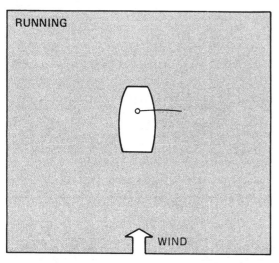

RUNNING

WIND

This boat is running

1 To run, begin on a reach.

2 Pull the tiller towards you so you turn away from the wind.

3 Then straighten up.

4 Let out the mainsheet until the boom is across the boat.

Where to sit when running

To begin, sit in the middle of the boat. As you gain confidence, tip (**kite**) the boat away from the boom.

The boat sails better if it is tipped so the sail is above it.

Be careful not to tip it too far!

Daggerboard

While you are learning, leave the daggerboard down when you are running. Later, you can pull it well up.

Gusts

If a gust hits you, try to keep going straight. Don't let it turn you round.

Steering

Be careful you don't pull the tiller towards you too much. If you do, the wind will blow into the sail from the other side and the boom will be pushed across with a bang. This is called a **gybe**. If this begins to happen, give the tiller a quick push, then straighten up.

10 Gybing

You have already learned to turn around by tacking. When you tack, you turn towards the wind. You can also turn the other way. This turn is called a gybe. The pictures show how you do it.

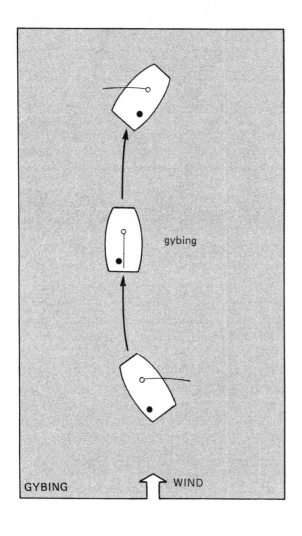

gybing

GYBING   WIND

1   Check to make sure you are on a run.

5   Pull the sail across, and duck.

2 Push the daggerboard half-down.

3 Grab all the parts of the mainsheet.

4 Pull the tiller towards you.

6 Straighten up.

7 Move across the boat facing forwards.

8 Change hands on the mainsheet and tiller.

11 Sailing a circular course

Sailing in a circle gives you practice on
each **point of sailing**.

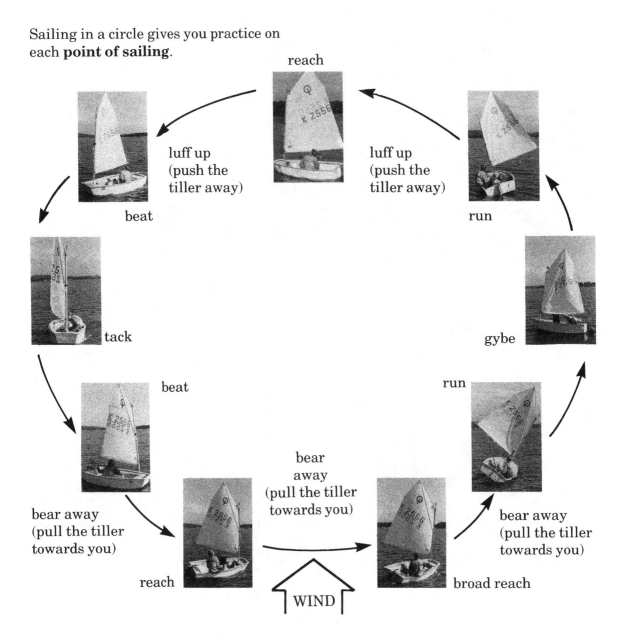

reach

luff up
(push the
tiller away)

luff up
(push the
tiller away)

beat

run

tack

gybe

beat

run

bear away
(pull the tiller
towards you)

bear
away
(pull the tiller
towards you)

bear away
(pull the tiller
towards you)

reach

broad reach

WIND

12 Safety

- You must be able to swim 25 metres without a lifejacket and float for 30 seconds.

- Always wear a buoyancy aid or a lifejacket when you are near water. Look after it – it could save your life one day. Make sure it is an approved type, fits properly, is fully inflated and correctly tied on.

- Never sail unless you've told someone you're going out.

- Check your buoyancy each time you go out. Don't sail if the bags are punctured.

- If you capsize, stay with the boat. Never try to swim ashore. It is further than it looks.

- If you need help, wave as shown in the pictures. (This is the international distress signal.)

Arms up.   **Arms out.**   **Arms down.**

- If you start feeling cold while out sailing, go ashore.

- Tie your mast to the boat so the rig doesn't fall out if the boat turns upside-down.

- You can't reef an Optimist. If the wind is too strong, you can take off the sprit and reduce sail (as shown in picture).

- Use a clip to fix the mainsheet to the boom. This is useful when landing and launching.

- Always take a bucket so you can bail out. Tie the bucket to the toestraps. A bucket that falls out isn't much help when you capsize. A small bailer is useful too, and so is a sponge.

- Carry a paddle to get you home if the wind drops.

- If you have long hair, tie it back or wear a hat. Otherwise it may get caught.

13 Capsizing

When you capsize, always stay with the boat.

1 Over you go!

2 Swim back to the boat.

3 Pull the daggerboard right down.

4 Grab it with both hands.

5 Put your feet on the side of the boat.

6 Now lever the boat half-way up.

7 Wait for the boat to turn and point into the wind.

8 Now put your feet on the daggerboard.

9 Grab the side of the boat and pull her upright.

10 Move towards the back of the boat and pull yourself over the side.

11 And sit down.

12 Bail out. If you are cold, sail home or wave for help.

14 Landing

Landing on a windward shore.

If the wind is blowing from the shore to the water, land like this:

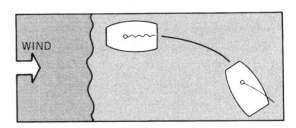

1 Beat towards the shore.

2 Let go of the mainsheet. Lift the daggerboard.

3 Now take out the rudder.

4 Unclip the mainsheet.

5 Jump out.

6 Ask a friend to bring the trolley.

7 Float the boat on to the trolley.

8 Pull them ashore.

Landing on a leeward shore

Land like this when the wind is blowing towards the shore:

  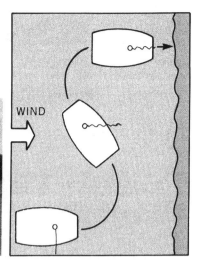

1 Sail towards the shore on a run.

2 Turn into the wind and unclip the mainsheet.

3 Turn back towards the shore.

4 Pull out the daggerboard.

5 Unclip the rudder.

6 Jump out.

7 Float the boat on to the trolley.

8 Pull them ashore.

15 What makes your boat sail?

When the wind blows from behind, your boat is pushed along like a feather on a pond. This is running.

But how does your boat sail across the wind (reaching), or sail towards the wind (beating)?

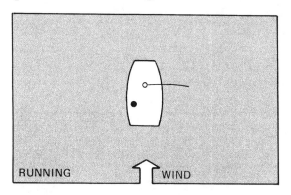

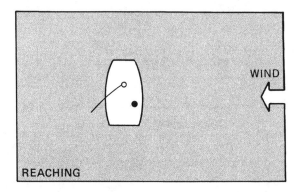

With the wind behind it, the boat is simply blown along.

With the wind blowing from the side, the boat is 'squeezed' forward.

The wind still pushes the sail, trying to make your boat slide sideways. But the daggerboard stops it sliding. It is rather like squeezing a piece of soap between your thumb (the wind) and your finger (the daggerboard). The pressure makes the soap shoot out, and in the same way a boat shoots forward through the water. The wind and the daggerboard also try to make your boat tip over (heel). But if you sit on the windward side, you will stop this, and your boat will move forwards.

This daggerboard is right down. It stops the boat sliding sideways.

This daggerboard is well up. Use it like this on a run.

16 Knots

Bowline
Use a bowline if you want to make a loop that will not slip.

Round turn and two half hitches
A safe way of tying a rope to a mooring ring or a post.

Single sheet bend
For joining two ropes of different thickness. Make the loop in the thicker rope first, then tie the knot as shown.

Figure of eight knot
Tie a figure of eight in the end of your sheet to stop it running out through the block.

 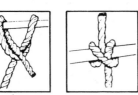

Clove hitch
For tying a rope to a railing or ring.

Whipping
Lay a loop of twine along the rope, then wind turns around tightly. Put the end through the loop and pull the other end. Finally cut off the ends.

 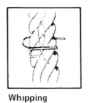

Rolling hitch
Use for tying your painter to a long towline.

Reef knot
For securing sail ties.

17　The rules

When several boats are on the water, they may crash unless there are rules about who has to keep out of the way. Here are two important rules to remember.

Windward boat gives way

If both boats are on the same tack, then the **windward** boat must keep clear. The windward boat is the one **nearer to the wind**. In this photo, the white boat is to windward, and must avoid the grey boat.

The white boat to windward must give way to the grey boat.

Port gives way to starboard

A boat is on **port tack** if the wind is blowing over its port (left) side. A boat is on **starboard tack** if the wind is blowing over its starboard (right) side. (Note: In the sailing rules, it is the custom to talk about a boat being on a 'tack' even though it may be beating, reaching or running.) If one boat is on port tack and the other is on starboard, then **port gives way to starboard**. In the photos, the white boat is on port tack and keeps clear of 'Hot Dog' which is on starboard tack.

18 Going faster

Adjusting the rig

1   **This sprit is too loose.**   2   **Pull it tighter.**

3   **Now the sail sets without creases.**

You will need to adjust the sail for various wind strengths. The following controls need altering:

- the sprit adjuster
- the kicking strap (vang)
- the outhaul
- the sail ties around the mast
- the mainsheet strop position

Strong winds

In strong winds you need everything very tight. It's best to set up the rig ashore with a friend helping you.

- The sail ties around the mast must be really tight otherwise a gap will open between the sail and the mast. Pull each tie tight and tie half a reef-knot (see page 40). Now ask a friend to put a finger on it to keep it tight while you finish the knot.

- The kicking strap (vang) and sprit work against each other, so you have to tighten them alternately, a little at a time. First pull on the kicking strap, then the sprit. Repeat, pulling them on one after the other until they are both tight.

- Start with the outhaul fairly tight. When you are sailing, you may find you can handle more power, in which case you can let off the outhaul a bit.

- Attach the mainsheet block towards the back (aft) end of the strop.

Light winds

- Adjust the sail ties until the sail just touches the mast.

- Tighten the sprit adjuster. Then let it off until all the creases disappear.

- To set the kicking strap (vang), pull in the mainsheet as you would for beating. Now pull the kicking strap until it is just tight, and cleat it.

- Surprisingly, you need the outhaul quite tight in light winds.

- The mainsheet should be attached to the centre of the strop.

Setting the mast rake

Attach a tape-measure to the top of your mast. Ask a friend to pull the mast back. While your friend is doing this, measure from the top of the mast to the middle of the top of the transom. Ask your friend to move the mast until the distance from the mast to the transom is between 270 and 275 cm. Your boat should now be well balanced (steer easily when beating).

If there is too much pull on the tiller when you're beating, point (**rake**) the mast forward. But rake the mast back if you need more 'feel'. Ideally, the boat should turn slowly into the wind if you let go of the tiller. This is **weather helm**. If the boat turns way from the wind when you let go of the tiller, you have **lee helm**. Cure this by raking the mast back.

FAST BEATING

Setting up the boat

- For beating, the sprit adjuster should be tight.

- The daggerboard should be right down. Use the elastic so the board is raked back in the water.

- Let out the mainsheet until the boom is above the corner of the transom

What you do:

- Sit in the middle of the boat. If you sit too far back, the transom drags through the water. If you sit too far forward, the bow will dig in. Move your body sideways to keep the boat flat.

- Steer with the tiller extension. This lets you move about and still control the rudder. *Hold the tiller extension across your body* so you can use your tiller hand to help adjust the mainsheet. (Never use your teeth to hold the mainsheet.) Watch the front of the sail carefully. Keep turning towards the wind until the sail begins to flap. Then pull the tiller and turn away until the sail just fills. You are now on course. Keep repeating this because the wind keeps altering its direction.

● Sometimes the wind shifts and you can turn towards it. This is a **lift** and is helping you get to the windward buoy. But sometimes the wind **heads** and you feel yourself sailing well away from the buoy. Now is the time to tack.

Watch the front of the sail.   **Keep the boat level.**

Beating in light winds

● Your burgee needs to be very sensitive.

● The sprit should be looser than normal.

● Let out the mainsheet until the boat begins to move. The boom may be out beyond the corner of the boat.

● Sit in front of the midship beam, with your feet behind it. Lean against the daggerboard case and move sideways until the boat is level. Sit still or you will shake the wind out of the sail.

● Don't tack too often because this slows you down.

Beating in strong winds

● Everything should be very tight.

● You may need to raise the daggerboard a little if you cannot keep the boat upright.

● Hike hard. Put your feet under the nearest toestrap. Lie back in an S shape with the edge (gunwhale) under your knees and your bottom resting against the side of the boat.

● If the bow digs in, move back. Otherwise sit just behind the midship beam.

● Use a ratchet block to help you hold the mainsheet. 'Clamp' the sheet between your hand and the edge of the boat (gunwhale). Only let out the mainsheet if the boat still heels when you are fully hiked.

● You may find a lot of water comes into the boat. Bail by holding the tiller and mainsheet in your back (aft) hand and the bailer in your front hand. Throw the water over your front shoulder.

FAST REACHING

As you bear away on to a reach, a lot of things need doing:

● Pull up the daggerboard about half-way. A good guide is to raise the board until the boom just clears it.

● Hold the mainsheet in your tiller extension hand, then move forward and let off the sprit adjuster about two or three inches. This puts shape into the sail.

- Don't try to adjust the other controls.

- Sit in the same place as you did on the beat – with your front leg against the midship beam. But move back if the bow digs in.

- If a gust hits you, lean back and give several pulls on the mainsheet. This is **pumping**.

- Take the mainsheet straight from the clip on the boom. It's much quicker to adjust the sail with a direct pull.

- Adjust the mainsheet so the sail flaps at the front (luff). Then pull in the mainsheet until the sail just stops flapping. **Telltales** (strips of wool or tape on each side of the sail) help here: adjust the sail until both telltales fly backwards. If the windward telltale (on the side of the sail nearer the wind) hangs down, pull in the mainsheet. If the leeward telltale (on the back of the sail) hangs down, let out the mainsheet.

Reaching in light winds

- Move forward a little and heel the boat towards the wind slightly.

- Let off the sprit to put even more fullness into the sail.

Reaching in strong winds

- There is no chance of moving forward to let off the sprit in strong winds. Leave it as it was on the beat.

- Move further back to lift the bow.

- Play the waves by moving your body. When the time comes to surf (**plane**) down a wave, lean out and back and pump the mainsheet.

- Watch for big gusts and try to turn away from the wind (**bear away**) before they hit you. Hike hard and pump the mainsheet to plane away from the gust before it has a chance to spin you round into the wind.

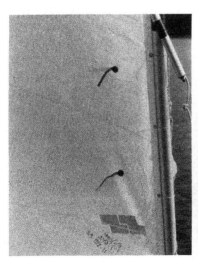

Fix the telltales to the sail like this.

Reaching in light winds.

Good, medium-wind reaching.

FAST RUNNING

- The sprit is the same as for the reach – as loose as possible without any creases in the sail.

- Pull up the daggerboard until none of it is in the water. (It is helpful to draw a line on the board to show you how far up it should be.)

- Make sure there is a knot in the mainsheet to stop the boom going out further than at right angles to the boat. Let out the mainsheet to this knot, but keep the end of the rope in your hand.

- Tip (kite) the boat to windward. To do this, sit on the side, facing forwards. Grab the toestrap with your mainsheet hand, lean back and pull the boat towards you. Stop when the water is running along the edge (gunwale).

- If the boat rolls, pull in the mainsheet hard and move quickly towards the other (leeward) side.

Kiting lifts the sail into stronger wind. It also lifts the flat bottom of the boat out of the water, which makes the boat go faster.

Running in light winds

- In light winds, the boom may not stay out when you kite the boat. So use the paddle to hold it out.

Kite the boat to windward to go faster on a run.

Running in strong winds

- For speed, have the daggerboard up. But it's safer (and slower!) to push it half-way down. This helps to stop the boat rolling.

- Pulling in the mainsheet also stops rolling (but slows you down).

- Sit well back to stop the bow nosediving. Keep the boat fairly flat – it is too dangerous to kite.

- There is no chance of letting off the sprit – leave it tight.

What's next?

Once you've learnt the basic skills, the best way of getting more from sailing is to join a club. If you haven't yet bought a dinghy, you should be able to sail with other club members or borrow club boats. That will help you to choose the right class of dinghy.

If you already have a dinghy, the sailing club will give you a base for your sailing and provide an introduction to racing, if that's what you want.

To find details about sailing clubs, you should contact your national authority for the sport. In the UK, that's the Royal Yachting Association. The RYA looks after every aspect of sailing, from training schemes for beginners to advice and help for experienced sailors and clubs.

Before you join a club, visit several to see exactly what they offer junior sailors. A well-organised club will have special activities for young people, which could include:

● Basic training
● Weekend camps
● Barbeques
● Visits to other clubs
● Race training
● Summer camps
● Fun days
● Open weekends

The junior fleet leader will be able to tell you more.

Another way of finding the right club is to contact the class association of the boat you want to sail. Every good class of dinghy has a lively national association made up of the people who sail that design. The Optimist, for example, has class associations in 47 countries. Each national association co-ordinates that country's club fleets.

For older sailors

When you move on from your first junior dinghy, exactly the same advice applies. If you can't decide what sort of boat will be best, your choice might be influenced by the fleets at your local club, as it's obviously better to select a popular class.

Learning more

Apart from training courses at sailing schools and clubs, the best way of keeping in touch is by reading one of the many yachting magazines. Each one is aimed at a certain section of the sport, so you can choose the one which interests you most.

Many dinghy sailors learn more from the large number of books on the sport, and Fernhurst Books provides a range of titles covering sailing from start to finish.

One thing is certain – once you start sailing, you've got a sport which will keep you involved for life. Good sailing.

Printed in the USA/Agawam, MA
November 30, 2010

555350.032